Things with Wings

THE LIFE CYCLE OF A
BAT

Gareth Stevens
PUBLISHING

by JoAnn Early Macken

Reading consultant: Susan Nations, M.Ed.,
author/literacy coach/consultant in literacy development

Please visit our website, www.garethstevens.com.
For a free color catalog of all our
high-quality books, call toll free
1-800-542-2595 or fax 1-877-542-2596.

Library of Congress Cataloging-in-Publication Data

Macken, JoAnn Early, 1953-
    The life cycle of a bat / by JoAnn Early Macken.
        p. cm. — (Things with wings)
    Includes index.
    ISBN-10: 0-8368-6379-8   ISBN-13: 978-0-8368-6379-6 (lib. bdg.)
    ISBN-10: 0-8368-6386-0   ISBN-13: 978-0-8368-6386-4 (softcover)
    1. Bats—Life cycles—Juvenile literature.   I. Title.
    QL737.C5M32   2006
    599.4—dc22   2005026539

Gareth Stevens Publishing
111 East 14th Street, Suite 349
New York, NY 10003

Copyright © 2006 by Gareth Stevens, Inc.

Managing editor: Dorothy L. Gibbs
Art direction: Tammy West
Photo research: Diane Laska-Swanke

Photo credits: Cover, p. 21 © Joe McDonald/Visuals Unlimited; p. 5 © James P. Rowan;
pp. 7, 9, 15, 17, 19 © Dietmar Nill/naturepl.com; p. 11 © Pete Oxford/naturepl.com; p. 13
© Rick & Nora Bowers/Visuals Unlimited

Printed in the United States of America

1 2 3 4 5 6 7 8 9 10 09 08 07

Note to Educators and Parents

Reading is such an exciting adventure for young children! They are beginning to integrate their oral language skills with written language. To encourage children along the path to early literacy, books must be colorful, engaging, and interesting; they should invite the young reader to explore both the print and the pictures.

Things with Wings is a new series designed to help children read about fascinating animals, all of which have wings. In each book, young readers will learn about the life cycle of the featured animal, as well as other interesting facts.

Each book is specially designed to support the young reader in the reading process. The familiar topics are appealing to young children and invite them to read — and re-read — again and again. The full-color photographs and enhanced text further support the student during the reading process.

In addition to serving as wonderful picture books in schools, libraries, homes, and other places where children learn to love reading, these books are specifically intended to be read within an instructional guided reading group. This small group setting allows beginning readers to work with a fluent adult model as they make meaning from the text. After children develop fluency with the text and content, the book can be read independently. Children and adults alike will find these books supportive, engaging, and fun!

— Susan Nations, M.Ed., author, literacy coach,
and consultant in literacy development

Bats are the only mammals that fly. Mammals give birth to live babies. The babies drink milk from their mothers.

A baby bat is born with no fur. It has to hold on to its mother or its **roost**, or resting place, until it learns to fly. A baby bat learns to fly when it is three or four weeks old.

baby bat

Most bats are active at night. During the day, they rest. They hang upside down by their feet. They also fold their wings around them.

feet

wings

9

Most bats live in caves. A cave can be crowded. Thousands of bats may live in one cave!

11

Bats can hear well. They use sound to find food. Some bats have round ears. Others have long ears.

ear

Most grown bats eat insects. They catch their food as they fly. One bat can catch hundreds of insects a night!

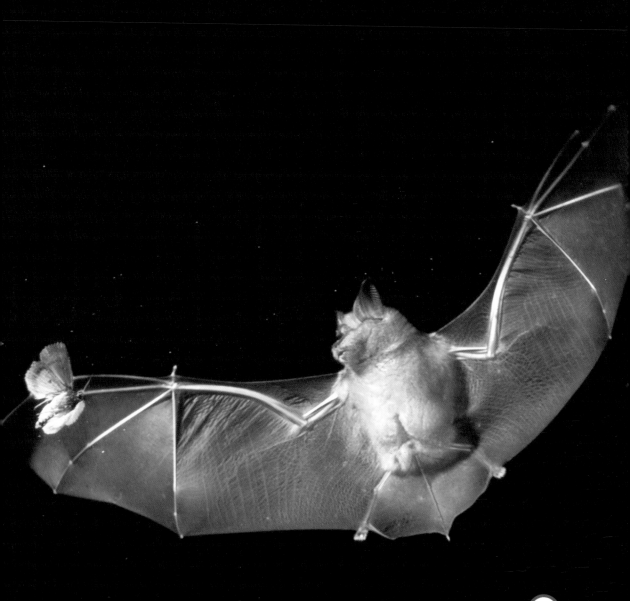

Some bats eat fruit. They feed at dawn and dusk. Their eyes are large so they can see their food in low light.

A few bats eat fish. A few bats eat frogs. Some bats bite cows, pigs, or other animals and drink their blood.

Some bats sleep through winter. Others **migrate**, or move, to warmer places. They come back in spring when they can find food. Then new babies are born. Some bats live for thirty years.

The Life Cycle of a Bat

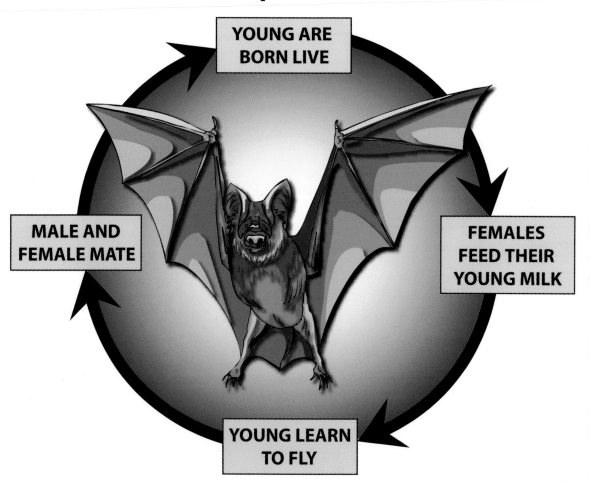

YOUNG ARE BORN LIVE

MALE AND FEMALE MATE

FEMALES FEED THEIR YOUNG MILK

YOUNG LEARN TO FLY

Glossary

dawn — the beginning of day

dusk — dim light at the beginning of night

mammals — animals that give birth to live babies and feed them milk

migrate — to move to a new place from time to time

roost — resting place

Index

About the Author

JoAnn Early Macken is the author of two rhyming picture books, *Sing-Along Song* and *Cats on Judy*, and more than eighty nonfiction books for children. Her poems have appeared in several children's magazines. A graduate of the M.F.A. in Writing for Children and Young Adults Program at Vermont College, she lives in Wisconsin with her husband and their two sons.